D1470115

Statue of Liberty

A Beacon of Welcome and Hope

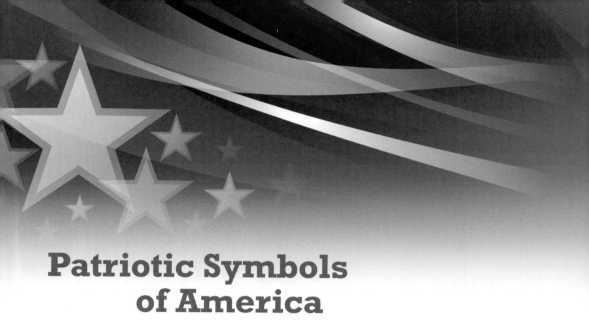

Patriotic Symbols
of America

Statue of Liberty
A Beacon of Welcome and Hope

Hal Marcovitz

Mason Crest
Philadelphia

Mason Crest
450 Parkway Drive, Suite D
Broomall, PA 19008
www.masoncrest.com

© 2015 by Mason Crest, an imprint of National Highlights, Inc.

Printed and bound in the United States of America.

CPSIA Compliance Information: Batch #PSA2014. For further information, contact Mason Crest at 1-866-MCP-Book.

Publisher's note: all quotations in this book come from original sources, and contain the spelling and grammatical inconsistencies of the original text.

First printing
1 3 5 7 9 8 6 4 2

Library of Congress Cataloging-in-Publication Data

on file at the Library of Congress

ISBN: 978-1-4222-3130-2 (hc)
ISBN: 978-1-4222-8753-8 (ebook)

Patriotic Symbols of America series ISBN: 978-1-4222-3117-3

Contents

KEY ICONS TO LOOK FOR:

Text-dependent questions: These questions send the reader back to the text for more careful attention to the evidence presented there.

Words to understand: These words with their easy-to-understand definitions will increase the reader's understanding of the text, while building vocabulary skills.

Series glossary of key terms: This back-of-the book glossary contains terminology used throughout this series. Words found here increase the reader's ability to read and comprehend higher-level books and articles in this field.

Research projects: Readers are pointed toward areas of further inquiry connected to each chapter. Suggestions are provided for projects that encourage deeper research and analysis.

Sidebars: This boxed material within the main text allows readers to build knowledge, gain insights, explore possibilities, and broaden their perspectives by weaving together additional information to provide realistic and holistic perspectives.

Patriotic Symbols and American History

Symbols are not merely ornaments to admire—they also tell us stories. If you look at one of them closely, you may want to find out why it was made and what it truly means. If you ask people who live in the society in which the symbol exists, you will learn some things. But by studying the people who created that symbol and the reasons why they made it, you will understand the deepest meanings of that symbol.

The United States owes its identity to great events in history, and the most remarkable of our patriotic symbols are rooted in these events. The struggle for independence from Great Britain gave America the Declaration of Independence, the Liberty Bell, the American flag, and other images of freedom. The War of 1812 gave the young country a song dedicated to the flag, "The Star-Spangled Banner," which became our national anthem. Nature gave the country its national animal, the bald eagle. These symbols established the identity of the new nation, and set it apart from the nations of the Old World.

To be emotionally moving, a symbol must strike people with a sense of power and unity. But it often takes a long time for a new symbol to be accepted by all the people, especially if there are older symbols that have gradually lost popularity. For example, the image of Uncle Sam has replaced Brother Jonathan, an earlier representation of the national will, while the Statue of Liberty has replaced Columbia, a woman who represented liberty to Americans in the early 19th century. Since then, Uncle Sam and the Statue of Liberty have endured and have become cherished icons of America.

Of all the symbols, the Statue of Liberty has perhaps the most curious story, for unlike other symbols, Americans did not create her. She was created by the French, who then gave her to America. Hence, she represented not what Americans thought of their country but rather what the French thought of America. It was many years before Americans decided to accept this French goddess of Liberty as a symbol for the United States and its special role among the nations: to spread freedom and enlighten the world.

This series of books is valuable because it presents the story of each of America's great symbols in a freshly written way and will contribute to the students' knowledge and awareness of them. It it to be hoped that this information will awaken an abiding interest in American history, as well as in the meanings of American symbols.

— Barry Moreno,
librarian and historian
Ellis Island/Statue of Liberty National Monument

Words to Understand

monarchy—undivided rule of a country by a member of a particular family.

monument—an object that serves to honor a person or event.

tyranny—oppressive power exerted by the government, where a single ruler has absolute power.

Sculptor Frédéric Bartholdi, the man who created the Statue of Liberty, used several women as models for the statue. One of them was his mother, Charlotte (inset).

The Face of Liberty

When the French sculptor Frédéric Auguste Bartholdi accepted the job of designing a huge *monument* to the cause of liberty, he faced an immense problem: How does one portray liberty?

He found his answer in America. During a visit to the United States in 1871, Bartholdi noticed that many American coins were engraved with a Roman goddess. Liberty, Bartholdi concluded, would be a woman.

Next, he borrowed heavily from a design he had conceived in 1869 while visiting Egypt, where the Suez Canal was under construction. The Suez Canal was a waterway that French engineers were digging. It would connect the Mediterranean and Red Seas. Bartholdi had proposed a giant statue of a woman holding a torch aloft to serve as a lighthouse at the canal's entrance, but the statue was never built.

Bartholdi thought the concept for the lighthouse would work in America. After all, the statue—which he decided to call "Liberty Enlightening the World"— would be erected in a harbor. So he tinkered with his design for the lighthouse. The American statue, he decided, would be the figure of a woman dressed in long robes holding a torch aloft to light the way. At her feet would be broken chains, to show that she had broken away from the bonds of *tyranny*. And she would hold a book of laws to symbolize America's devotion to the

VITAL FIGURE: Frédéric Bartholdi

Frédéric Auguste Bartholdi felt deeply about immigrants leaving their homes to make their lives in a new place because he had also lost his home. Bartholdi was born in 1834 in Colmar, a city in the Alsace region of France. During the Franco-Prussian War of 1870, France was beaten badly by the Germans and forced to give up some of its territory, including Alsace. Colmar and the remainder of Alsace would not be returned to France until after the Germans were defeated in World War I.

Following the Franco-Prussian War, Bartholdi lived in Paris where he worked as a prosperous sculptor. He got to know Édouard René de Laboulaye after being commissioned to carve a bust of the noted Paris intellectual. It was during dinner at Laboulaye's home that the idea first surfaced to produce a huge monument to American democracy.

After the dedication of the statue in 1886, Bartholdi returned to Paris, where he continued to work as a sculptor. He died in 1904.

common law. Printed across the law book would be the date July 4, 1776 (written in Roman numerals, July IV MDCCLXXVI), to commemorate the founding of the American republic.

Still, Bartholdi's design was not complete. All artists need models. For this job he turned to three women.

The first woman to sit as a model for the statue was the artist's fiancee, Jeanne-Émilie Baheux de Puysieux. Next, Bartholdi borrowed heavily from the features on the face of a woman in the painting "Liberty Leading the People," an 1855 creation by the French artist Eugène Delacroix depicting the image of a woman leading citizens in an uprising against the French *monarchy*. Finally, Bartholdi asked one more woman to sit as a model for his statue.

Years later, after the statue was finished, Bartholdi was joined at the Paris Opera by a member of the French Senate. Also attending the opera with Bartholdi was his mother, Charlotte Beysser Bartholdi. The senator later recalled, "I noticed an aged woman sitting in a corner. When the light fell on her face, I turned to Bartholdi and said to him, 'Why, that's your model for the Statue of Liberty!' 'Yes,' he answered calmly. 'It's my mother.'"

Text-Dependent Question
What painting did Bartholdi use as inspiration for the Statue of Liberty?

Research Project
Explain how the American Revolution inspired subsequent movements for liberty in France and other European countries.

 ## Words to Understand

ally—one that is associated with another as a helper.

colonists—a group of people who settle in a new land and form a community.

constitution—the document containing the laws that govern a country.

copper—a reddish-brown metal used mostly in pennies, as pipes for plumbing, and as electrical wire, but also used in sheets to make statues and parts of buildings.

democracy—a form of government in which the people of a nation select their own leaders and write their own laws.

ratify—to approve and sanction formally.

The Bastille, a French prison where political enemies of King Louis XVI were held, is attacked by an angry mob. The French Revolution began a few years after the American colonies won their freedom from Great Britain. The desire for democracy by many French people gave a writer named Édouard René de Laboulaye the idea of a monument to liberty.

Where Freedom Radiates

In the final years of the 18th century, the citizens of two nations won struggles to gain freedom from tyranny.

In America, the *colonists* rebelled against Great Britain. In 1776, they wrote the Declaration of Independence, which said that "all men are created equal." By 1783 the Americans had won their freedom. In 1789, the people of the young nation *ratified* the *Constitution*, a set of laws to "establish Justice, insure domestic Tranquility, provide for the common defence, promote the general Welfare and secure the Blessings of Liberty." The Constitution included a Bill of Rights, a set of rights guaranteed to every citizen of America that could never be taken away.

In Europe, the people of France won a similar victory. In 1789, the citizens rose up against King Louis XVI. During a bloody 10-year struggle the French installed a *democratic* government. They created a constitution quite similar to the one adopted in the United States.

But the French could not hold onto their liberty. The rule of the democratic French government soon fell into chaos and confusion. What's more, the government launched a number of unwise military actions against neighboring European nations. By 1799, the French experiment with democracy was over. An emperor named Napoleon Bonaparte had come to power, and the people of France were no longer free to pick their own leaders or make their own laws.

By 1865, Napoleon III, a nephew of Bonaparte, was in power. Soon, Napoleon III would start a war against Prussia, a region of Europe that is now part of Germany. In Paris, a college professor and writer named Édouard René de Laboulaye was angry at the stupidity of yet another French ruler. Laboulaye was a strong believer in democracy and a great admirer of the United States. He had written many books about America, and had urged his readers to follow the example of democracy that had succeeded across the Atlantic Ocean.

On an evening in 1865, Laboulaye sat down to dinner in his summer home near Versailles, France, with his friend, the sculptor Frédéric Auguste Bartholdi. During their dinner conversation, Laboulaye suggested that

France recognize the success of democracy in America. He wanted to build a huge monument to honor the idea of democracy, It could be a joint project by the two countries, Laboulaye said. After all, Laboulaye told Bartholdi, France had contributed greatly to the success of the American War of Independence. The French government had greatly aided the cause of liberty in America by sending 14 ships containing war supplies to the colonists. A French military leader, the Marquis de Lafayette, also traveled to America and lent his talents to

VITAL FIGURE: Édouard de Laboulaye

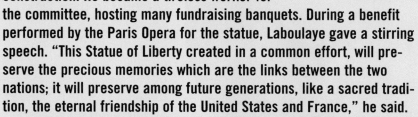

Édouard René Lefevbre de Laboulaye was the spiritual leader of the project to build the Statue of Liberty. It was at his home in Versailles in 1865 that the idea first surfaced.

Born in 1811, he was a writer and professor at the Institute of Sciences, Fine Arts, and Literature in Paris. He wrote many books on democracy and the United States, including a novel titled Paris in America.

Laboulaye was a founder of the Union Franco-Américaine, the committee in France that worked to raise $450,000 for the statue's construction. He became a tireless worker for the committee, hosting many fundraising banquets. During a benefit performed by the Paris Opera for the statue, Laboulaye gave a stirring speech. "This Statue of Liberty created in a common effort, will preserve the precious memories which are the links between the two nations; it will preserve among future generations, like a sacred tradition, the eternal friendship of the United States and France," he said.

Laboulaye did not live long enough to see the statue completed. He died in Paris in 1883, three years before the statue's dedication.

the Americans in their war against the British.

Bartholdi was intrigued by the notion of a monument to American liberty, but it would be six years before he actively took up the cause. Bartholdi had many other sculpting jobs to keep him busy.

In 1869, Bartholdi visited Egypt and came up with the idea of a lighthouse for the Suez Canal. He wanted to name this monument "Progress Bringing the Light to Asia." Although he showed drawings of his idea to the ruler of Egypt, the statue was never built.

Bartholdi continued to travel. In Vienna, Italy, he visited the shores of Lake Maggiore. There he saw an immense statue of St. Charles Borromeo, the 16th-century archbishop of Milan. The towering 76-foot statue was fashioned from thin sheets of *copper* fastened

The Marquis de Lafayette was a young officer in the French Army during the late 1770s. He took a small troop of soldiers to America, to help the colonists in their fight against British rule. Lafayette distinguished himself in the final battles of the Revolution, and the thankful colonists viewed him as a hero. Lafayette later returned to France and fought for freedom and democracy there.

to an internal framework of iron beams.

In 1870, Bartholdi returned to Paris to find France at war with Prussia. The Franco-Prussian War would be brief. France was soundly defeated and forced to give up territory to the conquering Prussians. One region taken by the Prussians was Alsace, the location of Bartholdi's home town, Colmar. France's loss meant the end of the reign of Napoleon III. The nation once again became a democratic republic.

After the humiliation of the Franco-Prussian War, and with the French people uncertain how to govern themselves, the time seemed ripe to Laboulaye to revive his idea of a monument to democracy. And so, in 1871 he turned to his friend Bartholdi to make it happen.

He urged Bartholdi to visit the United States and find out whether Americans would be interested in a project undertaken by the two nations. "Go to see that country," he told the sculptor. "Propose to our friends over there to join with us in making a monument."

Bartholdi soon left for the United States, sailing across the Atlantic on the ocean liner *Pereire*. He arrived in New York Harbor on June 21. For five months, he traveled across the United States, visiting cities from New York to San Francisco. He met Horace Greeley, the influential publisher of the *New York Tribune*, and William Curtis, the editor of *Harper's Weekly*, the leading news magazine of the 19th century. He sat down with President Ulysses S. Grant at Grant's summer home in

Long Beach, New Jersey. Grant was cordial and listened carefully to Bartholdi's plans, but did not offer the help of the United States government to the project.

In Philadelphia, Bartholdi made an important friend when he met with Colonel John W. Forney, publisher of the *Philadelphia Press*, an influential newspaper. Forney was very interested in the project, and over the next few years would prove to be a valuable *ally*.

Make Connections

In August 1876 the name "Statue of American Independence" was registered by Bartholdi at the U.S. Copyright Office; it was assigned number 9939 of 1876.

In Boston, Bartholdi found another ally in Henry Wadsworth Longfellow, the popular poet. "He showed great enthusiasm for my project," Bartholdi said. "When I left he shook my hand so warmly and firmly I had the feeling that he wanted to shake hands with all of France."

Bartholdi continued his travels. By train, he visited a dozen more cities, including Hartford, New Haven, Niagara Falls, Washington, D.C., St. Louis, Cincinnati, Detroit, Chicago, Denver, Omaha, Salt Lake City, and San Francisco. The sculptor later said he could not help but be impressed with the sweeping landscape of America. "One enters valleys and gorges, one passes through trenches and tunnels, from one ravine to the other, skirting enormous masses of rocks," he wrote. "Some of the sights are magnificent."

After five months of traveling and meeting with political leaders, bankers, industrialists, literary figures, publishers, and ordinary citizens, Bartholdi was convinced the American people were enthusiastic about his plans for the statue. But he found himself returning to Paris with no firm commitment from anybody to raise money for the project, which was sure to be expensive.

The trip to America did produce one important development. On June 21, 1871, as he sailed into New York Harbor aboard the *Pereire*, in what Bartholdi described as "the pearly radiance of a beautiful morning," the ship passed what was known then as Bedloe's Island. Bartholdi knew instantly that the island would be the perfect location for his statue.

He wrote in his diary: "I have the feeling that it is here that my statue should be. Here where men have their first glimpse of the New World; here where freedom radiates."

Text-Dependent Question
How did France contribute to the success of the patriots during the American War for Independence?

Research Project
Explain the causes of the Franco-Prussian War, and how this conflict impacted the French people, as well as the rest of Europe in the late 19th and early 20th centuries.

 Words to Understand

architect—a person who designs buildings.

centennial—a 100th anniversary.

engineer—a person skilled in applying scientific knowledge in the construction of a building or large structure.

journalism—the craft of writing news for publication in a newspaper or magazine, or for broadcast on radio or television.

landmark—a well-known figure or part of the landscape.

lottery—a drawing of lots, governed by chance, used to decide something.

Visitors to the Philadelphia Centennial Exhibition, held in the summer of 1876, were fascinated by the 30-foot arm and torch of the statue. Bartholdi had originally hoped to have the statue ready for the centennial, but soon realized more time and money were needed to complete the work. After the exhibition ended, the arm and torch were displayed in New York's Madison Square Garden from 1877 to 1882.

The New Colossus

Although Bartholdi did not receive money from the Americans, his reception had been so warm in the American cities that he returned to France with enthusiasm for the project. Back in Paris, Bartholdi and Laboulaye forged ahead with their plans. In 1874, they formed the Union Franco-Américaine, a committee to head the project in France. The goal of the committee was to present "Liberty Enlightening the World" to the American people on July 4, 1876, the 100th anniversary of the signing of the Declaration of Independence.

Bartholdi and Laboulaye found their French countrymen willing to open their pockets. But they soon realized their deadline was too ambitious. The money would never be raised and the statue completed in time for the *centennial* of American democracy. Still, plans moved forward.

In America, boosters of the project were also working hard to raise money. It had been decided early on that although the project would be a joint effort involving the two countries, the statue itself would be a gift from the French people to America. The Americans would, therefore, be responsible for designing, building, and, of course, paying for the massive pedestal that would be needed on Bedloe's Island. In America, that job fell to an organization that called itself the American Committee on the Statue of Liberty. The committee was formed on January 2, 1877, and headed by William M. Evarts, a lawyer and political leader from New York.

In May 1876, Bartholdi left Paris to make a second trip to America. He planned to attend the Philadelphia Centennial Exhibition, a world's fair celebrating the 100th anniversary of the United States. That summer, Bartholdi was joined at the exhibition by a "visitor" from France that would cause quite a sensation in America and provide a treat for fairgoers: the 30-foot arm of the statue holding the "Torch of Liberty." Before leaving Paris, Bartholdi had started work on the statue. The arm and torch were finished in time for the fair in Philadelphia. The entire statue was far from complete, but Bartholdi did manage to provide a piece of his creation by the original July 4, 1876, deadline.

The arm and torch delighted fairgoers in Philadelphia

as well as citizens of New York, where the segment was also put on display. Colonel Forney's newspaper in Philadelphia issued a challenge to New York: if the city to the north could not find the money for the

Make Connections

The French raised money for the project by hosting banquets inside the statue while it was being fashioned in Bartholdi's workshop; the first banquet featured dinner for 25 people inside Miss Liberty's kneecap.

pedestal, Philadelphia would be happy to accept the statue. During the next few years, San Francisco, Boston, and Cleveland would make similar challenges.

But New Yorkers were smitten with the statue. Thousands lined up and paid 50 cents to scale a ladder erected inside the arm while it was on display in Madison Square on Fifth Avenue.

The people who climbed the ladder inside the arm and took a close look might have noticed how the statue was constructed. Bartholdi knew the statue would need a strong skeleton to withstand the wind and weather of New York Harbor. He recalled his trip some years before to Italy and his visit to the 76-foot statue of St. Charles Borromeo: the statue had been made of copper and fastened to an interior framework of iron. Now, Bartholdi decided to copy that method for Miss Liberty, which was planned to be much taller—she would rise 151 feet 1 inch from the base to the tip of the torch.

The copper would be shaped and riveted to the iron

frame in sheets no thicker than 3/32 of an inch. Bartholdi knew a lot about molding copper, but he would need help designing and erecting the massive iron framework. For that job, he turned to a famous French *engineer*, Alexandre Gustave Eiffel. Known as the "iron magician," Eiffel had made his reputation as a designer of railroad bridges. Years later, following the completion of the Statue of Liberty, Eiffel built France's most famous *landmark*, the 900-foot Eiffel Tower in Paris.

Together, the two men worked to create what was now known as the "Statue of Liberty" in a huge workshop Bartholdi rented in Paris. They supervised dozens of laborers, who first formed the segments of the statue from thin strips of wood. The copper was carefully shaped around the wooden forms in gentle hammer blows, then

A French engineer named Alexandre Gustave Eiffel designed the iron skeleton of the Statue of Liberty. A few years after the statue was completed, Eiffel built France's most famous landmark, the Eiffel Tower.

transferred to an identical metal framework that Eiffel had designed. During the late 1870s and early 1880s, hundreds of Parisians visited the workshop on Sundays, when it was open to the public. They watched the statue rise into the air, becoming part of the colorful Paris cityscape until it was finally completed. Then it was taken apart in sections and packed in crates for transportation aboard ship to New York.

Make Connections

Small versions of the Statue of Liberty are on display in Paris at Luxembourg Gardens and on the Seine River.

In America, the project had hit some bumps in the road. Although the public greeted the arrival of the arm and torch with fascination and enthusiasm, newspaper editors were still regarding the project with skepticism. An editorial in one newspaper said: "Although the arrival of the statue's arm may seem to be a satisfactory token to show that the remainder of the statue will soon follow, sensible people favor an opposing theory: If Bartholdi had honestly intended to complete a statue, then he would have started at the base."

And the *New York Times* suggested that the statue and pedestal could cost as much as $2 million—a very large amount of money for a public project in those times. The newspaper questioned whether such a large sum could ever be raised by the citizens of France and America.

Still, the American Committee pressed on. By 1877, the committee was actively raising money for the statue and met with so much early success that the U.S. Congress voted to formally accept the Statue of Liberty as a gift from the people of France and permit Bartholdi to use Bedloe's Island for the project. Organizers of the American fundraising effort received more encourage-ment when an image of the statue was featured in a painting by the American artist Edward Moran titled *Liberty Enlightening the World's Commerce*. The painting featured a golden Miss Liberty standing tall out of a misty fog in New York Harbor, surrounded by boats whose sailors raise their hats in salute. The painting was taken on tour and hung in banquet halls where the American Committee held its fundraising dinners.

In Paris, the Union Franco-Américaine held a number of its own banquets, sold models of the statue, and staged *lotteries* featuring valuable prizes to raise money. In time, the Union succeeded in raising the $450,000 Bartholdi needed to complete the statue.

In America, the project was lagging again. By March 1883 the American Committee had raised about $150,000 and was still $100,000 short of the funds needed to erect the pedestal. Evarts asked Congress for the money, but the nation's lawmakers flatly refused to commit public funds to the project.

News of the American Committee's failure to raise the remainder of the money arrived at the desk of Joseph Pulitzer, publisher of the *New York World*. Pulitzer was one of the nation's most influential newsmen. He felt deeply about the symbol of democracy the Statue of Liberty would represent. He decided to use the power of his newspaper to raise the remainder of the money. On March 14, 1883, the *New York World* launched a campaign to raise the rest of the money for the pedestal.

"The Bartholdi statue will soon be on its way to New

Newspaper publisher Joseph Pulitzer (inset) used the power of the *New York World* to raise $100,000 to help build the pedestal of the Statue of Liberty. This copy of the August 11, 1885, *World* front page triumphantly announces that the goal has been reached. Pulitzer was an immigrant himself. He had been born in Hungary in 1847, and came to America in 1864. Pulitzer is most remembered as one of the founders of "Yellow *Journalism*," a style of news reporting that reported scandalous stories using bold headlines to attract attention. The Pulitzer Prize is an award presented annually to the creators of the best work in American journalism and literature.

York. The great goddess comes with a torch held aloft to enlighten the world," read the first of what would be many editorials.

At first, the money trickled in. After two months, just $135.75 had been donated by readers of the *World*. But Pulitzer kept up the pressure. "Money must be raised to complete the pedestal for the Bartholdi statue," the newspaper wrote. "It would be an irrevocable disgrace to New York City and the American Republic to have France send this splendid gift without our having provided even so much as a landing place for it."

For months, the *World* continued making pleas for funds. Anybody who sent in money would have his or her name published in the *World*. Slowly, the readers responded. One young office boy from New York gave five cents. "As being loyal to the Stars and Stripes, I thought even five cents would be acceptable," he said. A little girl sent in $1. She said, "I will always be proud that I began my career by sending you $1 to aid in so good a cause."

Finally, on August 11, 1885, the *New York World* ran this banner headline: "One Hundred Thousand Dollars! Triumphant Completion of the World's Fund for the Liberty Pedestal." With money in hand, the American Committee turned its attention to completing the pedestal. That job was assigned to an **architect** named Richard Morris Hunt.

The cornerstone for the pedestal had been laid on

VITAL FIGURE: Architect Richard M. Hunt

By the time Richard Morris Hunt was asked to design the pedestal for the Statue of Liberty, the architect had made his reputation as the designer of the luxurious mansions on fashionable Fifth Avenue in New York.

Hunt was born October 31, 1827, in Brattleboro, Vermont. Until he tackled the problem of how to make the statue stand tall, Hunt's work mainly centered on how to display the wealth and power of America's richest people. But the pedestal for the Statue of Liberty would be a much different project: Hunt had to design a structure to support a steel-and-copper giant that weighed more than 150 tons. What's more, his creation would become part of what would be regarded as the welcoming beacon for America's newest, and poorest, citizens.

Among his other creations are the Lenox Library, the facades of the Metropolitan Museum of Art and the Tribune Building in New York, the Marquand Chapel at Princeton University in New Jersey, the Scroll and Key Club at Yale University in Connecticut, and the Yorktown Monument in Virginia.

Richard Morris Hunt died in 1895. Three years later, a memorial to Hunt was unveiled in New York's Central Park, facing the Lenox Library.

August 5, 1884. It was a six-ton block of granite, cut from a quarry in Leete, Connecticut. Placed inside the cornerstone was a copper box containing a number of items, including a coin minted in 1824, the year the Marquis de Lafayette last visited the United States.

The pedestal was built inside the star-shaped walls of Fort Wood, which had been erected on Bedloe's Island during the War of 1812 to protect New York against British invasion. By the time Bartholdi saw it on his first visit to New York in 1871, the fort had long since lost its strategic importance and was by then used mostly for storage. On the 12-acre island, Hunt erected a pedestal standing 154 feet tall, containing 54 million pounds of poured concrete.

There was one final detail. In 1883, to help raise money for the project, the American Committee had sponsored an exhibition of art and poetry. One of the

VITAL FIGURE: Poet Emma Lazarus

The Colossus of Rhodes was a giant statue that towered over the harbor of a Greek island 2,300 years ago. Although it was destroyed in an earthquake, the Colossus served as an inspiration to Emma Lazarus, the poet whose moving words have been engraved in bronze and attached to the base of the Statue of Liberty.

Lazarus gave her poem "The New Colossus" to the American Committee on the Statue of Liberty, which was seeking a poem to be read at the monument's dedication. The committee chose a poem written by John Greenleaf Whittier instead. Still, the noted American writer James Russell Lowell made his feelings known when he told her: "I liked your sonnet about the statue much better than I liked the statue itself."

Emma Lazarus was born in 1849 in New York City, the daughter of wealthy Jewish parents. At 18, she met the poet Ralph Waldo Emerson, who praised her poetry. Later, she became an important literary voice supporting the plight of oppressed people, particularly Jewish citizens of Russia persecuted by the government of the czar, the ruler of Russia.

Lazarus was in London when the Statue of Liberty was dedicated. While in England, she developed cancer. She returned home to New York, where she died on November 18, 1887, at the age of 38.

The New Colossus

Not like the brazen giant of Greek fame,
   With conquering limbs astride from land to land;
Here at our sea-washed, sunset gates shall stand
   A mighty woman with a torch, whose flame
Is the imprisoned lightning, and her name
   Mother of Exiles. From her beacon-hand
Glows world-wide welcome; her mild eyes command
   The air-bridged harbor that twin cities frame.
"Keep, ancient lands, your storied pomp!" cries she
   With silent lips. "Give me your tired, your poor,
Your huddled masses yearning to breathe free,
   The wretched refuse of your teeming shore.
Send these, the homeless, tempest-tost to me,
   I lift my lamp beside the golden door!"

poems submitted for the exhibition was written by Emma Lazarus, the daughter of a wealthy New York family. The poem, titled "The New Colossus," received little recognition when it was first published, but it soon came to be identified closely with the statue. In 1903, it was engraved onto a bronze plaque and permanently attached to the pedestal.

Text-Dependent Question
What New York newspaper publisher used his influence to raise funds for the Statue of Liberty?

Research Project
Using your local library or the Internet, find out more about the origins of the star-shaped base of the Statue of Liberty. Why was it built in this pattern?

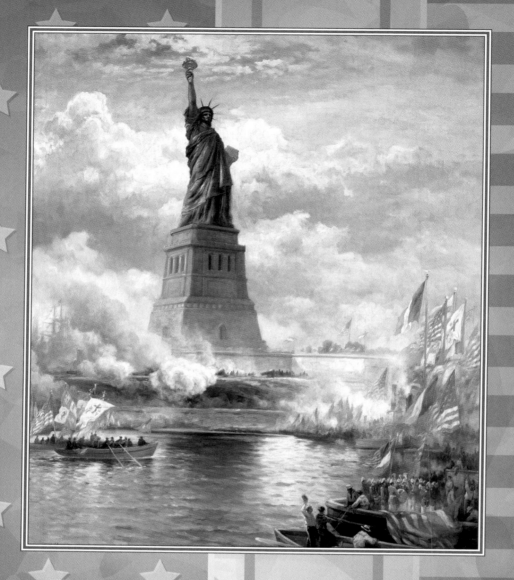

 Words to Understand

patina—a green film that forms on copper when it is exposed to the weather.

scaffolding—a temporary structure erected outside or inside a building to support workers while they build or repair the structure.

The Statue of Liberty was unveiled on October 28, 1886. Hundreds of boats streamed past the statue in New York Harbor, blowing their horns. President Grover Cleveland concluded the ceremony by saying, "We will not forget that Liberty has made here her home, nor shall her chosen altar be neglected."

"My Daughter Is Here"

When the Statue of Liberty arrived at Bedloe's Island in New York Harbor, it hardly looked like the towering national symbol familiar today to most Americans. In fact, when the statue arrived it was packed in 214 crates. It took 16 days for longshoremen in Rouen, France, to load the freighter *Isère* with the crates containing the statue. The *Isère* arrived at Bedloe's Island on July 22, 1885.

"Finally, the most solemn moment," wrote Bartholdi. "My daughter is here! Every boat around began sounding their whistles, but in America whistles don't whistle, they roar or howl. Never have I heard a more gigantic concert. The ceremony was followed by a 100-gun salute. It was wonderful."

When it was completed, the statue weighed a total of 156 tons. That includes the copper sheeting, which weighs 62,000 pounds, and the steel framework inside, which weighs 250,000 pounds. The weight of the concrete pedestal is 54 million pounds.

The statue stands 151 feet 1 inch from the base to the tip of the torch, and 305 feet 1 inch from the ground to the tip of the torch. The length of Miss Liberty's hand is 16 feet 5 inches; her index finger is eight feet long. Her head measures 17 feet 3 inches from her chin to the top of her crown, and 10 feet across from ear to ear. The length of an eye is 2 feet 6 inches. Her nose is 4 feet 6 inches long.

Visitors to the Statue of Liberty climb 353 steps to get to the crown—or they can take the elevator. Inside the crown, visitors will find 25 windows, symbolizing the 25 gemstones of the Earth. The crown has seven points, representing the seven continents and seven seas of the world.

The reason the statue is green is that copper, when exposed to the weather, takes on a green tint. This is known as a *patina*.

The Statue of Liberty was renovated in the 1980s. Among the costs were $2 million to replace the torch; $5.3 million to reinforce Miss Liberty's shoulder and erect a new viewing platform inside the crown; $1.8 million to power-wash the statue inside and outside to remove stains caused by 100 years of leaking seams in the copper; $3.3 million to replace the 1,825 steel bars

The statue is owned by the federal government and maintained by the National Park Service. In the 1980s, it underwent a major renovation.

and 12,000 rivets that tie the copper skin to the internal skeleton; $1.2 million to install a glass elevator; $8.7 million for a new lobby to the Museum of Immigration in the pedestal as well as $4 million for new exhibits in the museum; $1.1 million for new plumbing, ventilation, and heating systems for the museum; $3.5 million for water-proofing the statue, and $2.5 million to erect the *scaffolding* that the workers needed during the renovation.

When the renovated statue was dedicated on July 4, 1986, millions of people flooded into New York to take part in the four-day "Liberty Weekend" extravaganza.

 Text-Dependent Questions
How tall is the Statue of Liberty? How much does the statue weigh?

 Research Project
The final cost of the Statue of Liberty was $700,000 in 1885. Using an online inflation calculator, find out what that cost equates to in present-day dollars. Then compare that figure to the total renovation cost listed in this chapter.

 Words to Understand

bond—an interest-bearing certificate of money owed by the government to the holder of the bond.

doughboy—an American soldier in World War I. The name stems from the buttons on their uniforms; they resembled dumplings, which are cooked from dough.

intolerance—the state of being unwilling to grant social or political rights.

Immigrants on the ocean liner *Olympic* cheer as their ship steams past the Statue of Liberty. For more than 100 years, the statue in New York Harbor has been a proud symbol of American freedom and democracy.

The Symbol of America

Although immigration from European countries to America started as long ago as 1607, when the first colonists arrived at Jamestown, Virginia, about one-third of the population of the United States today—roughly 110 million people—is directly related to the immigrants who passed the Statue of Liberty on their way to Ellis Island between 1892 and 1954.

More than 12 million immigrants arrived at Ellis Island during those years. One of them was Mary Antin, who arrived aboard the ocean steamer *Polynesia* in 1893. The 12-year-old Jewish girl and her family immigrated to the United States to escape religious *intolerance* in Polotzk, Russia. In 1912, she wrote the book *The Promised Land*. As her ship approached New York Harbor, Antin wrote, "One of us espied the figure and face we longed

37

to see for three long years. In a moment, five passengers on the *Polynesia* were crying, 'Papa!'"

Another immigrant was Edward Corsi, who first saw the statue in 1907. Here is how Corsi, who later became commissioner of the immigrant processing center at Ellis Island, described his first vision of Miss Liberty:

> This symbol of America—this enormous expression of what we had all been taught was the inner meaning of the new country we were coming to—inspired awe in the hopeful immigrants. Many older persons among us, burdened with a thousand memories of what they were leaving behind, had been openly weeping ever since we entered the narrower waters on our final approach toward the unknown. Now somehow steadied, I suppose, by the concreteness of this symbol of America's freedom, they dried their tears.

The Danish poet Adam Dan had this to say as his boat passed the statue: "We came not empty-handed, but brought a rich cultural inheritance."

The Statue of Liberty has served as a symbol of America's cultural diversity since its dedication in 1886. But it has also become a symbol of freedom. In 1917, as America's *doughboys* left to fight in World War I, the United States government raised money for the war by selling Liberty *Bonds*. Advertisements encouraging citizens to buy the bonds often featured an image of the Statue of Liberty. On one poster, Miss Liberty points out to the viewer and says, "You buy a Liberty Bond lest I perish!" Also, doughboys in America's "Liberty

This dramatic poster was one of many created during the First World War to feature the Statue of Liberty as a symbol of American freedom.

THAT LIBERTY SHALL NOT PERISH FROM THE EARTH
BUY LIBERTY BONDS
FOURTH   LIBERTY   LOAN

Division" were issued helmets with an image of the Statue of Liberty.

In 1936, Americans celebrated the 50th anniversary of the statue. It was a dark time for democracy in Europe and beyond. Tyrants had come to power in Germany, Italy, and Japan. Soon those nations would be at war with the free people of the world. On October 28, 1936, President Franklin Delano Roosevelt spoke at a ceremony for the anniversary of the statue. He said:

> Fifty years ago our neighbor and friend across the sea gave us this monument to stand at the principal eastern gateway to the New World. Grover Cleveland, president of the United States, accepted this gift with the pledge that "we will not forget that liberty has here made her home; nor shall her chosen altar be neglected." During those 50 years that covenant between ourselves and our most cherished convictions has not been broken.

During the 1950s, the patterns of immigration to the United States changed. With the development of air

A harbor fire tug shoots streams of colored water into the air during the centennial celebration of the Statue of Liberty in 1986.

transportation, immigrants were now more likely to arrive aboard an airplane than by boat. Ellis Island was closed in 1954. No longer would the towering figure of Miss Liberty greet newcomers as they saw their first glimpses of America from the deck of an ocean liner.

The Statue of Liberty has become a national landmark, seen by more than 4 million visitors a year. In 1956, Congress changed the name of the statue's home from Bedloe's Island to Liberty Island. In 1972, the Museum of Immigration was opened to the public. In 1982, President Ronald Reagan created the Statue of Liberty-Ellis Island Centennial Commission to raise money for extensive renovations of the statue, as well as to Ellis Island. Both the statue and Registry Hall, the cavernous immigration depot on Ellis Island, had fallen victim to neglect and the elements. The commission raised $87 million for the repairs.

On July 4, 1986, the nation held a grand birthday

KEY EVENT: Closures of the Statue

The Statue of Liberty has been closed to the public several times in recent years. After the September 11, 2001, terrorist attacks the statue, and other American monuments like Independence Hall, were closed for security reasons. The pedestal reopened to visitors in 2004. The statue itself was opened to visitors on July 4, 2009.

In 2011, the Statue of Liberty was closed for a year so that safety features, including a new staircase, could be installed. It reopened in October 2012, but soon closed again due to the effects of Hurricane Sandy. The hurricane caused major damage to the infrastructure of Liberty Island. The statue opened again on July 4, 2013.

In early October 2013 the Statue of Liberty, like other national parks, was closed for about two weeks due to a government shutdown.

party for Miss Liberty. Millions of Americans flooded into New York City to take part in the celebration.

One of those Americans was Mario Cuomo, governor of the state of New York. Cuomo had grown up on the streets of Queens, part of New York City. He was the son of immigrants who had come through Ellis Island.

"For me and for millions of New Yorkers, the Statue of Liberty feels like an old friend," Cuomo said. "Her presence is familiar, constant, comforting. We feel a tremendous pride that she's stood beside this Golden Door."

Text-Dependent Question

How many immigrants passed the Statue of Liberty on their way to Ellis Island between 1892 and 1954?

Research Project

What were the security concerns that caused the Statue of Liberty to be shut down from 2001 to 2009? Have they been alleviated, and if so, how?

Chronology

1865 Frédéric Auguste Bartholdi, a sculptor, and Édouard René de Laboulaye, a writer and college professor, conceive the idea of a monument to American democracy.

1869 Bartholdi visits Italy, where he observes the statue of St. Charles Borromeo, which is fashioned from copper sheets attached to an iron framework.

1874 The Union Franco-Américaine forms to support the project in France.

1876 The arm holding the torch of the Statue of Liberty is unveiled at the Philadelphia Centennial Exhibition July 4.

1877 On January 2, the American Committee on the Statue of Liberty forms to back the project in the United States.

1883 On March 14, newspaper publisher Joseph Pulitzer starts a two-year campaign to raise $100,000 for the pedestal.

1884 The cornerstone for the statue is laid on Bedloe's Island on March 14.

1885 The statue, contained in 214 crates, arrives at Bedloe's Island on a ship from France on July 22.

1886 On October 28, the Statue of Liberty is unveiled and dedicated in a grand ceremony in New York City attended by President Grover Cleveland.

1903 The poem "The New Colossus" by Emma Lazarus is engraved onto a plaque and affixed permanently to the base of the statue.

1986 On July 4, the renovated Statue of Liberty and Ellis Island are re-dedicated in a ceremony.

2001 The statue is closed following the September 11 terrorist attacks. The pedestal is reopened in 2004, with visitors not allowed into the statue until 2009.

2012 Hurricane Sandy causes major damage to the infrastructure of Liberty Island. The statue is closed until July 2013.

Series Glossary

capstone—a stone used at the top of a wall or other structure.

cornerstone—the first stone placed at a spot where two walls meet, usually considered the starting point of construction.

dome—an element of architecture that resembles the hollow upper half of a sphere.

edifice—a large building with an imposing appearance.

facade—the decorative front of a building.

foundation—the stone and mortar base built below ground that supports a building, bridge, monument, or other structure.

hallowed—holy, consecrated, sacred, or revered.

keystone—the architectural piece at the crown of a vault or arch which marks its apex, locking the other pieces into position.

memorial—something designed to help people remember a person or event in history.

obelisk—a shaft of stone that tapers at the peak.

pantheon—a public building containing monuments to a nation's heroes.

pedestal—the base or support on which a statue, obelisk, or column is mounted.

portico—a roof supported by columns, usually extending out from a building.

rotunda—a large and high circular hall or room in a building, usually surmounted by a dome.

standard—a flag or banner that is adopted as an emblem or symbol by a nation.

symbol—an item that represents or stands for something else.

Further Reading

Berenson, Edward. *The Statue of Liberty: A Transatlantic Story*. New Haven, Conn.: Yale University Press, 2012.

Boyer Binns, Tristan. *The Statue of Liberty*. Crystal Lake, Ill.: Heinemann Library, 2001.

Heinrichs, Ann. *The Statue of Liberty*. MInneapolis: Compass Point Books, 2001.

Cuomo, Mario. "I've Watched the Lady All My Life Now." *Life*, July 1986.

Kent, Deborah. *The Statue of Liberty*. New York: Scholastic, 2012.

Moreno, Barry. *The Statue of Liberty Encyclopedia*. New York: Simon and Schuster, 2000.

Shea, Pegi Deitz. *Liberty Rising: The Story of the Statue of Liberty*. Illus. by Wade Zahares. New York: Henry Holt, 2013.

Rappaport, Doreen. *Lady Liberty: A Biography*. Illus. by Matt Tavares. Somerville, Mass.: Candlewick Press, 2008.

Internet Resources

http://www.nps.gov/stli

This National Park Service website is the official site for the Statue of Liberty, and provides information about the park, history of the statue, and links to photos and multimedia.

http://www.statueofliberty.org

Website of the Statue of Liberty-Ellis Island Foundation, established in 1982 to raise money to renovate the statue. Today the foundation remains dedicated to restoration, preservation, and education at the Statue of Liberty and Ellis Island.

http://whc.unesco.org/en/list/307

Information on the Statue of Liberty from the United Nations Educational, Scientific, and Cultural Organization (UNESCO).

http://www.nyctourist.com/liberty1.htm

This site provides information for tourists interested in visiting the Statue of Liberty

Index

Index

Picture Credits

Contributors

BARRY MORENO has been librarian and historian at the Ellis Island Immigration Museum and the Statue of Liberty National Monument since 1988. *The Statue of Liberty Encyclopedia* (2000), *The Encyclopedia of Ellis Island* (2004), *Ellis Island's Famous Immigrants* (2008), and *The Ellis Island Quiz Book* (2011). He also co-edited a scholarly study on world migration called *Leaving Home: Migration Yesterday and Today* (2011). His biography has been included in *Who's Who Among Hispanic Americans*, *The Directory of National Park Service Historians*, *Who's Who in America*, and *The Directory of American Scholars*. Mr. Moreno lives in New York City.

HAL MARCOVITZ has written more than 100 books for young readers. He lives in Chalfont, Pennsylvania, with his wife, Gail. They have two grown daughters, Ashley and Michelle.